P9-DDG-971
FROM OUR FRONT PORCH
Chef Williams' Cajun Injector™

Photo by Ron Dobbs

To Edgar Williams

"From Our Front Porch" is a fitting dedication to my late husband Edgar and our life together of 43 years. As you prepare these recipes and share them with friends and family, I hope they bring you as much joy and satisfaction as they brought Edgar and me. The inspiration for these dishes came from his love of people, food and entertaining. From Log Cabin Fried Chicken, to the Front Porch Restaurant, to Cajun Injector, we've fed many thousands in groups of one to hundreds. Many of these recipes will become your family's favorites...

Edgar would have liked that.

For the past 25 years, we have been treating the friendly folks of south Louisiana to our own special recipe for cooking meat Cajun style.

Photo by Ron Dobbs

Edgar and Reece

The tradition began, as many traditions do, at our home in Clinton, Louisiana. Celebrations have always been a big part of Cajun culture, and they became especially important when they provided us the chance to get together with family and friends in our kitchen. Thus, the marinade was born.

Word soon spread to neighbors. From area hunters to ski slope vacationers — everybody wanted to take Edgar's seasonings with them. Local charities even had special fund-raisers featuring Edgar's delicious food.

Edgar, myself and our son, Reece, then decided to open the soon-to-be-famous Front Porch restaurant. Our menu featured many wonder-

Mary, Reece, Jeanne and Edgar at QVC's "Quest for the Best" show

Reece and Edgar displaying "Best of Show" award.

ful dishes, some of which you can experience from this book, but the house specialty was our prime rib. People from all over the world came to feast on this truly unique tasting dish.

In 1979, just two short years after opening, The Front Porch was named the "Restaurant of the Year" by the Louisiana Tourist Commission. This award was given mainly because of other numerous awards we had received for our prime rib, which was injected with what is now the Cajun Injector beef, pork and wild game marinade, "Cajun Aujus" (the Creole Garlic recipe).

Our family sold the restaurant in 1982 and began to toy with the idea of bottling our marinades for home use. Finally, in 1987, Cajun Injector, Inc. was born.

Edgar got to see the success of our family's growing business venture. In 1993, the A.C. Neilson Ratings rated the Cajun Injector marinades and marinating system as the most popular marinades in the deep south, which strengthened our product's popularity. In 1995, during QVC's "Quest for America's Best: 50 in 50 Tour," Cajun Injector was chosen as Louisiana's "Best of the Show" on the 24 hour shopping network. Since then, we have been a regular guest on the show, appearing on QVC networks airing in England, Scotland, Ireland and the United States. (Later we were awarded 2nd runner up for QVC's hottest selling products during 1995.) That same summer, Cajun Injector was approached by Entrepreneur Magazine. Our family-owned business was featured in the June 1995 edition's cover story of "Million Dollar American Success Stories."

Our family continues to carry on the cooking tradition since Edgar passed away in November, 1995. Through this cookbook and future ventures, we look forward to feeding and entertaining people worldwide for years to come.

Reece off-camera at QVC

Reece injecting marinade for a Baton Rouge television show.

Photo by Ron Dobbs

FROM JEANNE WILLIAMS

Thank you for asking about our cookbook, "From Our Front Porch."

Compiling it has almost been like raising a child. It was extra hard getting these dishes together, since we never have used recipes and trained our kitchen staff without them. I've spent three years, cooking, correcting, pushing and prodding it into the kind of cookbook I've always wanted. Now, I want you to enjoy it too. I made it to be used, not just take up space. I hope you like it.

This is one time that "too many cooks spoil the soup" is not true. It took the hard work, time and devotion of all of these people, and to them I am very grateful.

First and always to "God," for giving me the strength and knowledge to keep going.

To my late husband, Edgar, for his sense of humor, his love of life and his love of people.

To my son, Reece and his wife Mary, whose support, knowledge, leadership in running the company, and belief that I could do it, helped me go on.

To QVC for allowing us to present this collection world-wide.

To Theresa Shea, cookbook designer and typesetter, who became a very patient friend.

To my daughters, Diane and Aline, and my son Ron, who have always been my biggest supporters (and critics)., whose shoulders have always been there for me.

Maureen and Betsy Jones, help in writing Edgar's dedication.

Kay Andrews and Carolyn Sessions for critiquing my recipes and letting me know "if the chicken is supposed to go in a pan before you wrap it, you must say so."

And to everyone else involved, and you know who you are!

INJECTING TECHNIQUES FOR CHICKEN

IMPORTANT: Pour marinade into separate container before injecting to keep from contaminating marinade.

CHICKEN

BAKED

1: Remove giblets and rinse turkey with warm water. Drain cavity completely.
2: Attach needle to Cajun Injector by turning clockwise until snug. Do not over-tighten needle.
3: Pour needed marinade into separate container and draw into Injector.
4: Inject turkey with following amounts at points indicated on illustration.
Points A: Inject FULL Injector (approximately 1-1/4 oz.) into each breast. Insert Injector at an angle completely into each breast. Push plunger down slowly while pulling Injector slowly out of meat. This gives even distribution of seasoning.
Points B: Inject FULL Injector into both points on each thigh using same technique.
Points C: Inject FULL Injector into each drumstick.
5: Sprinkle outside of turkey generously with *Cajun Shake*™ (seasoned salt) – rub in well.
6: Bake in conventional manner

MICROWAVE

1: Follow steps 1-4 (BAKED)
5: Sprinkle outside of chicken generously with *Cajun Shake*™ (seasoned salt) and paprika (for added color).
6:. Place in microwave-proof dish. Cover with film wrap punched with several holes. Cook on full power for 9 minutes per pound — rotating dish several times.

DEEP FRIED:

1: Follow steps 1-4 (BAKED)
5: Sprinkle outside of chicken generously with *Cajun Shake*™ (seasoned salt). (Do not add paprika.)
6:. Caution: Make sure all water is drained from cavity before deep frying. Deep fry whole chicken in one gallon of oil at 350° F for 9 minutes per pound.

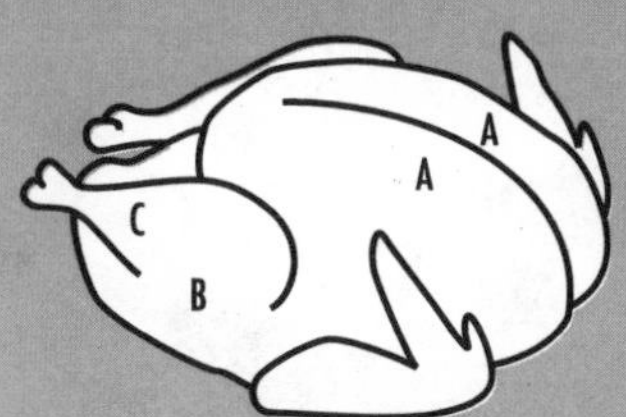

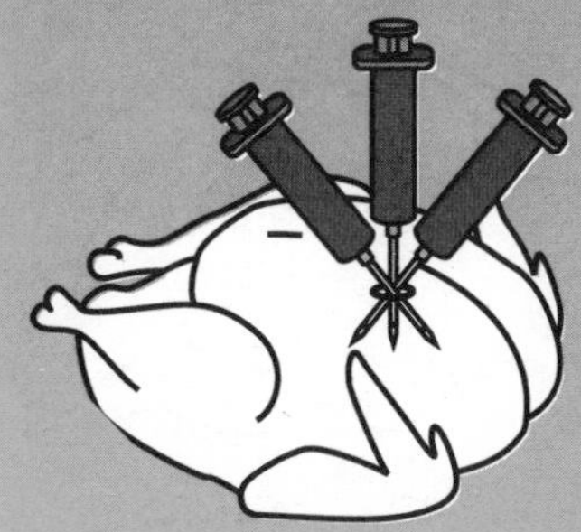

For best results, insert Injector at different angles through same hole when injecting at each point indicated.

CLEANING & STORAGE:

Clean Injector with soap & warm water. Allow to dry then lightly coat rubber tip of plunger with vegetable oil. This allows plunger to move freely in barrel.

INJECTING TECHNIQUES FOR TURKEY & ROAST

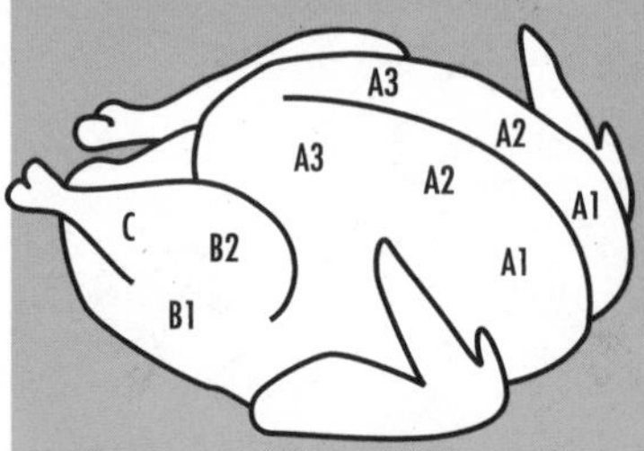

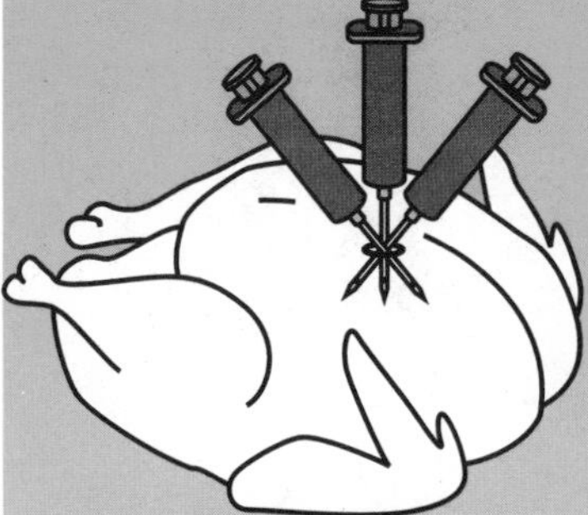

For best results, insert Injector at different angles through same hole when injecting at each point indicated.

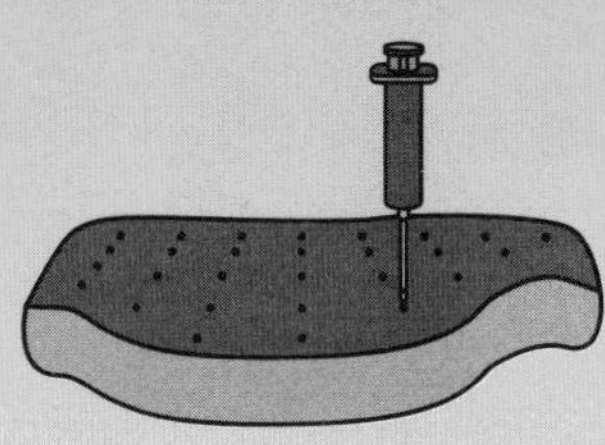

On thick cuts of meat, it is best to inject from both sides.

TIP: Add Cajun Injector Marinade Original Recipe for beef to bloody mary mix for a great spicy drink.

TIP: Put Cajun Shake on popcorn.

TURKEY

1: Remove giblets and rinse turkey with warm water. Drain cavity completely.
2: Attach needle to Cajun Injector by turning clockwise until snug. Do not over-tighten needle.
3: Pour needed marinade into separate container and draw into Injector.
4: Inject turkey with following amounts at points indicated on illustration.
Points A1, A2 & A3: Inject FULL Injector (approximately 1-1/4 oz.) into each side of breast at each point indicated. Insert Injector at an angle completely into each breast. Push plunger down slowly while pulling Injector slowly out of meat.
Points B1 & B2: Inject FULL Injector into both points on each thigh using same technique.
Points C: Inject FULL Injector into each drumstick.
5: Sprinkle outside of turkey generously with *Cajun Shake*™ (seasoned salt) – rub in well.
6:. Caution: Make sure all water is drained form cavity before deep frying. Deep fry whole turkey in 3-4 gallons of oil at 350° F for 3-1/2 minutes per pound. Or bake in conventional manner.

BEEF, PORK & WILD GAME

1: Attach needle to Cajun Injector by turning clockwise until snug. Do not over-tighten needle.
2. Pour needed marinade, 2 oz. per pound of meat, into separate container and draw into Injector.
3: Place roast in pan and inject marinade at points every 1 - 2 inches apart (see illustration). Insert Injector completely. Push plunger down slowly while pulling Injector slowly out of meat. This gives even distribution of seasoning.
4: Pour marinade generously over roast.
5: Cook in oven until desired temperature is reached.

TABLE OF CONTENTS

RECIPES

BEEF, PORK & LAMB

Cajun Sidebar:

This is the original recipe that won the awards and accolades that the Front Porch Restaurant was famous for.

When injecting any meat, make sure that the marinade is used generously throughout. Cajun Injector has many marinades to try...or use one of your own creations.

INGREDIENTS	
8	**lbs. boneless beef top round**
16	**fl. oz. Cajun Injector Beef Marinade (Creole Garlic recipe)**

EDGAR'S CAJUN AUJUS BEEF

This is the technique that made the "Front Porch Prime Rib" famous.

Serves 16 (approx.)

Attach needle to Cajun Injector by turning clockwise until snug. DO NOT OVER TIGHTEN NEEDLE.

Pour marinade (2 oz. per pound of meat) into separate container and draw into injector.

Place roast into 2-3 inch deep pan and inject marinade at points every 1-2 inches apart. After injecting, pour generous amounts of marinade over roast. Cover with foil and bake at 350 degrees until desired temperature is reached. (You can cook this outside on the pit also.)

A whole rib-eye or prime rib done this way is wonderful!

NUTRITION INFORMATION PER SERVING

Calories	Saturated Fat	Total Fat	Protein	Carbohydrates	Cholesterol	Sodium
274	2.6g	7.5g	51.7g	0.0g	129mg	118mg

Cajun Sidebar:

Beef brisket is best when cooked slowly for many hours. Keeping the meat covered with foil and injected with our marinades will produce a succulent, cut-it-with-your-fork entree.

Calories and fat percentages will vary depending upon how much fat you trim off the brisket.

Cajun Beef Brisket

INGREDIENTS	
12	lbs. beef brisket, trimmed
2	16 fl. oz. jars Cajun Injector Beef Marinade (Creole Garlic recipe)

Serves 24 (approx.)

Trim all fat from brisket before starting.

Inject 2 to 3 oz. marinade per pound of meat. Place roast in a 2-3 inch deep pan and cover with foil. Cook at 350 degrees for approximately 3 1/2 hours or until tender. Remove foil and brown for 15 minutes.

NUTRITION INFORMATION PER SERVING

Calories	Saturated Fat	Total Fat	Protein	Carbohydrates	Cholesterol	Sodium
695	24.2g	60.2g	38.4g	0.0g	166mg	145mg

Cajun Sidebar:

If you're serving a lot of guests, make this recipe the day before and freeze the patties, wrapping them separately. Defrost before grilling and serve JB's potato salad (see "Sides & Salads") along with it!

TIP:
PUT CAJUN SHAKE ON POPCORN.

INGREDIENTS

- ☞ **lean ground beef**
- ☞ **Cajun Injector marinade (Creole Garlic recipe)**
- ☞ **Italian bread crumbs**

MARY'S CAJUN BURGERS

Serves Everybody!

Grill up as much as you need. Just adjust the following formula to feed one or one hundred:

Use 4 tbsp. of Cajun Aujus, and 2 tbsp. of Italian bread crumbs per pound of ground beef.

Mix ingredients well. Mold into patties and fry or grill to desired doneness.

NUTRITION INFORMATION PER SERVING

Calories	Saturated Fat	Total Fat	Protein	Carbohydrates	Cholesterol	Sodium
n/a	n/a	n/a	n/a	n/a	n/a	n/a

Cajun Sidebar:

The key to this recipe is searing the outside of the roast before cooking. This will let all of the natural juices and garlic work its flavor on the meat.

INGREDIENTS	
5	lbs. beef rump roast
☞	garlic
☞	Cajun Shake to taste
1/2	cup vegetable oil
1/2	cup flour
4	cups water (apprx.)

MY SUNDAY POT ROAST

Every Sunday we looked forward to Mama's pot roast, rice and gravy, and English peas.

Serves 10 (approx.)

Cut slits in roast with a small, sharp knife. Peel garlic, and insert half a clove into slit. Make as many slits as you like garlic (the more the better).

Rub the outside of roast with Cajun Shake, making sure that some gets into the slits that you have made. (Salt and black pepper may be substituted for Cajun Shake.)

Cover the bottom of a large black iron pot or heavy, large dutch oven with vegetable oil and heat until hot. Place roast in oil and sear on all sides. Remove from pot and set aside.

Make a roux by adding flour to the drippings left in the pot. After roux is brown, add enough water to almost half cover the roast. Cover and cook for 1 1/2 to 2 hours or until done and tender.

NUTRITION INFORMATION PER SERVING

Calories	Saturated Fat	Total Fat	Protein	Carbohydrates	Cholesterol	Sodium
276	3g	8g	52g	0g	129mg	118mg

Cajun Sidebar:

Serve this pork loin roast along with our recipe for candied yams listed in the Sides, Salads & Sauces section

INGREDIENTS

- ☞ **boneless pork loin roast (5-6 lbs.)**
- ☞ **Cajun Injector's Poultry Marinade (Creole Butter recipe)**

Serves 12

Fill injector with Cajun Injector's Poultry Marinade, or try using half beef marinade (Creole Garlic recipe) and half poultry marinade (Creole Butter recipe).

Inject the roast generously and grill or bake at 325 degrees until desired temperature is reached.

NUTRITION INFORMATION PER SERVING

Calories	Saturated Fat	Total Fat	Protein	Carbohydrates	Cholesterol	Sodium
400	9g	25g	44g	1g	145mg	176mg

Cajun Sidebar:

This ham recipe is sure to please a hungry holiday crowd. For a tangy marinade, replace the prepared mustard with Creole mustard.

Honey Ham Glaze

INGREDIENTS	
1/4	cup honey
1/4	cup catsup
2	tsp. onions, minced
2	tsp. Cajun Injector marinade (Creole Garlic recipe)
2	tsp. prepared mustard
1/4	tsp. grated lemon peels
1/8	tsp. ginger
5-6	lbs. pre-cooked ham

Serves 12

Place whole cloves in rows or a pattern in top of ham. Place on rack in shallow baking pan. Mix together all ingredients and spread on top and sides of ham. Bake in 350 degree oven about one hour. Serve hot or cold.

NUTRITION INFORMATION PER SERVING

Calories	Saturated Fat	Total Fat	Protein	Carbohydrates	Cholesterol	Sodium
286	3.6g	10.9g	42.4g	4.6g	98mg	2956mg

Cajun Sidebar:

Barbequing marinated beef tip roast on the pit gives this recipe a country smoked flavor.

INGREDIENTS

☞	**beef tip roast (6-8 lbs.)**
16	**fl. oz. Cajun Injector's Red Wine Marinade**

Red Wine Beef

Serves 12

Shake marinade well. Place roast in a 2-3 inch deep pan.

Inject roast with 1 to 2 oz. in several places evenly around roast. 16 oz. will do a 6-10 lb. roast nicely.

Pour a generous amount of the Red Wine Marinade over the roast. Cover with foil. Cook in oven at 350 degrees or on pit with meat thermometer until desired temperature is reached.

NUTRITION INFORMATION PER SERVING

Calories	Saturated Fat	Total Fat	Protein	Carbohydrates	Cholesterol	Sodium
407	4g	13g	66g	0g	164mg	511mg

Cajun Sidebar:

Rosemary-Garlic marinade also works well when injected into whole chickens.

INGREDIENTS	
6-8	**lbs. pork loin**
16	**fl. oz. Cajun Injector's Rosemary-Garlic Marinade**

Serves 12

Fill injector with Cajun Injector's Rosemary-Garlic Marinade. Inject roast (using 2 oz. per pound) in several places evenly around roast.

Place roast in 2 inch pan and bake in oven at 325 degrees until desired temperature is reached. (Approximately 1 hour with pre-heated oven.)

This is excellent grilled on the pit outside, without the pan.

NUTRITION INFORMATION PER SERVING

Calories	Saturated Fat	Total Fat	Protein	Carbohydrates	Cholesterol	Sodium
367	6g	16g	50g	5g	143mg	857mg

Cajun Sidebar:

This recipe also works well on the grill. Baste regularly to keep the lamb's outside surface from drying out.

INGREDIENTS	
6 1/2	lbs. leg of lamb
☞	lemon juice
☞	Cajun Injector's Rosemary-Garlic Marinade

Roast Leg of Lamb

Serves 8

Preheat oven to 400 degrees.

Inject Cajun Injector's Rosemary-Garlic Marinade in leg of lamb using approximately 1-1/2 to 2 oz. per pound.

Rub fresh lemon juice and a little black pepper evenly over the surface.

Place leg of lamb in a roasting pan and put it in the oven. Immediately reduce heat to 350 degrees. Roast 1-1/2 hours for medium rare.

NUTRITION INFORMATION PER SERVING

Calories	Saturated Fat	Total Fat	Protein	Carbohydrates	Cholesterol	Sodium
422	5g	15g	70g	1g	218mg	921mg

Cajun Sidebar:

A perfect summer-time recipe, shish kebabs are a pleasant break from the traditional outdoor feasts. Vary the recipe by adding a combination of meats, vegetables and even fruit!

INGREDIENTS	
1 1/2	lbs. lamb, cubed
☞	cherry tomatoes
☞	sweet green pepper cut into 1 inch squares
☞	small white onions, peeled
1	oz. Cajun Injector's Red Wine Marinade
1	oz. Cajun Injector's Rosemary-Garlic Marinade

LAMB KEBABS

Serves 6

Use about 1 oz. Cajun Injector's Red Wine Marinade mixed with about 2 oz. Cajun Injector's Rosemary-Garlic Marinade. Pour over lamb cubes and marinate refrigerated for 2 hours.

Remove lamb from marinade. Slide onto skewers, alternating with 2 cherry tomatoes, a square of green pepper, and a small white onion.

Broil for about 10 minutes, basting with reserved marinade until done. Serve immediately.

NUTRITION INFORMATION PER SERVING

Calories	Saturated Fat	Total Fat	Protein	Carbohydrates	Cholesterol	Sodium
148	2g	6g	23g	1g	73mg	218mg

Cajun Sidebar:

Wrapping steaks in plastic wrap before injecting marinade is a "neat" trick. This also works for chicken and fish filets as well.

REECE'S GRILLED STEAK

INGREDIENTS

- ☞ **8-10 oz. rib eye**
- ☞ **Cajun Injector's Beef Marinade (Creole Garlic recipe or Red Wine flavor)**

Serves 1

Completely wrap steak in plastic wrap (this keeps the marinade from getting everywhere). Fill the injector with Cajun Injector's Beef Marinade and inject the steak in several places. Remove the plastic wrap and grill to desired doneness.

NUTRITION INFORMATION PER SERVING

Calories	Saturated Fat	Total Fat	Protein	Carbohydrates	Cholesterol	Sodium
324	6g	16g	45g	0g	134mg	148mg

Cajun Sidebar:

A never-fail recipe, this meat loaf will be a family favorite. Cajun Aujus and Cajun Shake add a rich flavor without making the dish too spicy.

Creole Garlic Meat Loaf

INGREDIENTS	
3	lbs. lean ground beef
1	whole onion, chopped
3	cloves garlic, chopped
1	cup seasoned bread crumbs
2	whole eggs
1/2	cup milk
8	fl. oz. Cajun Injector marinade (Creole Garlic recipe)
☞	Cajun Shake to taste

Serves 8

Mix meat, onions, garlic, Cajun Shake, bread crumbs, eggs, milk and 2 oz. Cajun Injector Marinade in bowl. When thoroughly mixed, mold into a loaf.

Place in lightly greased 2-3 inch deep baking pan.

Inject in several places 2 oz. Cajun Injector Marinade into meat loaf and pour remainder over loaf.

Bake at 350 degrees for 1 to 1 1/2 hours or until meat is done.

NUTRITION INFORMATION PER SERVING

Calories	Saturated Fat	Total Fat	Protein	Carbohydrates	Cholesterol	Sodium
525	15g	38g	34g	13g	184mg	317mg

POULTRY

Cajun Sidebar:

Deep frying whole birds is becoming a holiday tradition. To test how much oil to use, fill the pot with water and lower the bird into the pot. Mark the kettle at the point where the water covers the bird. Empty the water, and fill the pot with oil to that line. Make sure the bird is dry and defrosted before frying.

FRENCH FRIED CHICKEN

INGREDIENTS	
3	**lbs. fryer chickens**
☞	**Cajun Injector Poultry Marinade (Creole Butter Recipe)**
☞	**Cajun Shake**

Serves 6

Remove giblets from fryer, rinse with warm water, pay dry and leave whole.

Inject with Cajun Injector Poultry Marinade several places in breast, thighs and legs. Use about 4 oz. per chicken.

Sprinkle Cajun Shake over bird and inside cavity.

Deep fry whole at 350 degrees for 9 minutes per pound, using about one gallon of oil.

NUTRITION INFORMATION PER SERVING

Calories	Saturated Fat	Total Fat	Protein	Carbohydrates	Cholesterol	Sodium
470	9.6g	33.6g	41.6g	0.3g	204mg	159mg

Cajun Sidebar:

You can gauge the amount of oil to use by following the instructions outlined on the French Fried Chicken sidebar. Turkey cooked with this method turns out more succulent and flavorful than oven baked birds.

CAUTION:

WE DO NOT RECOMMEND USING A TURKEY WEIGHING MORE THAN 12 POUNDS.

CAJUN FRIED TURKEY

Once you've eaten a turkey prepared this way, chances are you will not want another baked one. You won't have any left-overs with this recipe, and that's a promise.

INGREDIENTS	
12	lb. turkey
☞	Cajun Injector Poultry Marinade (Creole Butter Recipe)
☞	Cajun Shake

Serves 18

Remove giblets from turkey, rinse with warm water, pat dry (especially inside cavity) and leave whole.

Inject 4 oz. of Cajun Injector Poultry Marinade on each side of breast. Inject approximately 2 oz. in each leg and thigh. Use about 16 oz. per turkey.

Rub Cajun Shake over bird and inside cavity.

Hold bird by legs and lower (breast first) slowly into oil. **MAKE SURE ALL WATER IS DRAINED FROM CAVITY BEFORE PLACING BIRD INTO THE OIL.**

Deep fry whole in 3 - 4 gallons of oil (preferably peanut oil) at 350 degrees for 3 1/2 minutes per pound.

NUTRITION INFORMATION PER SERVING

Calories	Saturated Fat	Total Fat	Protein	Carbohydrates	Cholesterol	Sodium
476	7g	24g	62g	3g	206mg	1030mg

Cajun Sidebar:

I don't use microwaves except to warm food — however, this is a "real winner."

Microwaving chicken is quick and easy to clean up after. It also keeps the heat down in the kitchen on those hot, summer days.

CHICKEN IN A "FLASH"

INGREDIENTS

2 1/2	**lb. fryer chickens**
☞	**Cajun Injector Poultry Marinade (Creole Butter Recipe)**
☞	**Cajun Shake or paprika**

Serves 6

Remove giblets from fryer and rinse.

Inject with Cajun Injector Poultry Marinade several places in breast, thighs and legs. Use about 4 oz. for 2 1/2 lb. bird.

Sprinkle Cajun Shake on outside. Place in microwave-safe dish and cover with plastic wrap. Make several holes in wrap to allow steam to escape.

Microwave on high setting, cooking 8 minutes per pound. Turn midway through cooking period.

NUTRITION INFORMATION PER SERVING

Calories	Saturated Fat	Total Fat	Protein	Carbohydrates	Cholesterol	Sodium
392	8g	28g	35g	0g	170mg	132mg

Cajun Sidebar:

The Cajun Injector Rosemary-Garlic marinade is great way to give a bland chicken a boost.

INGREDIENTS	
2 1/2	**lb. fryer chickens**
☞	**Cajun Injector Rosemary Garlic Marinade**
☞	**paprika**

Rosemary/Garlic Chicken

Serves 6

Clean fryer.

Inject fryer with Rosemary Garlic marinade, using about 4 oz. Inject in several places in breast, thighs and legs. Sprinkle outside of fryer with paprika.

Place fryer in microwave-safe dish, cover with plastic wrap (make several holes in film to let steam escape). Microwave on high for 8 minutes per pound, turning midway through cooking time.

You can also bake this fryer in the oven. Use the same method except you do not have to sprinkle with paprika or cover with plastic wrap.

NUTRITION INFORMATION PER SERVING

Calories	Saturated Fat	Total Fat	Protein	Carbohydrates	Cholesterol	Sodium
392	8g	28g	35g	0g	170mg	132mg

WILD GAME

Cajun Sidebar:

This recipe works well with alligator, too. Cube the alligator meat and follow the recipe to the right.

Wild Duck Sauce Piquante

INGREDIENTS	
3	ducks, cut in pieces
☞	lemon juice
8 oz.	Cajun Injector marinade (Creole Garlic recipe)
4	onions, finely chopped
☞	cooking oil
1	bell pepper, finely chopped
4	stalks celery, chopped
8 oz.	can tomato sauce
6 oz.	can tomato paste
5	garlic cloves minced
1	bunch green onions, chopped
1	bunch parsley, chopped
1	small can water chestnuts, drained and chopped

Serves 24 (approx.)

Soak ducks overnight in a solution of 1 part vinegar to 1 part water.

In a heavy iron pot, brown ducks in a small amount of oil. Remove ducks from pot and set aside. Add marinade, bell pepper,, celery, tomato sauce, tomato paste, 1/2 of the green onions, parsley and just enough water to keep mixture from sticking to pot. Cover and cook slowly for 1½ hours, stirring often to prevent sticking.

Add ducks to cooked sauce and cook another 1½ hours.

Add water chestnuts and remaining green onions and parsley just before serving. Serve over rice.

NUTRITION INFORMATION PER SERVING

Calories	Saturated Fat	Total Fat	Protein	Carbohydrates	Cholesterol	Sodium
654	21g	62.5g	19g	4g	120.5mg	108mg

Cajun Sidebar:

The back strap is the prime piece of venison to use.

INGREDIENTS

1/4	cup sherry
5	lb. venison roast
1	lb. carrots (2" lengths)
1	lb. quartered onions
1	lb. quartered potatoes
1	lb. bacon
8-10	oz. Cajun Injector marinade (Creole Garlic recipe)

VENISON MAURICE

Serves 10

Inject roast with the marinade and place in a 2 inch deep pan. Arrange bacon on top of roast. Place cut vegetables around roast. Pour sherry over roast and veggies.

Cover and cook at 350 degrees for 90 minutes (time may vary depending on oven).

To brown, remove cover 30 minutes before roast is done.

NUTRITION INFORMATION PER SERVING

Calories	Saturated Fat	Total Fat	Protein	Carbohydrates	Cholesterol	Sodium
685	12.5g	33.5g	74.6g	19.7g	284mg	475mg

Cajun Sidebar:

This venison recipe is "melt in your mouth" delicious.

SMOKED VENISON

INGREDIENTS	
8	lbs. venison roast
16	oz. Cajun Injector Beef Marinade (Creole Garlic recipe)
4	oz. melted butter
☞	Crystal Hot Sauce

Serves 10

Melt butter and add to marinade. Inject

2 - 3 ounces of marinade and butter mixture per pound of venison. Rub outside of roast with Crystal Hot Sauce. Cook on smoker to desired doneness.

NUTRITION INFORMATION PER SERVING						
Calories	Saturated Fat	Total Fat	Protein	Carbohydrates	Cholesterol	Sodium
496	9.2g	18g	83.4g	0.0g	333mg	279mg

Cajun Sidebar:

If duck is not available, substitute chicken and add sliced italian sausage to the recipe.

INGREDIENTS

2	ducks, cut into serving pieces
2	quarts water
1/2	cup cooking oil
1/2	cup flour
1	onion, diced
2	stalks celery, diced
1	small bell pepper, diced
1/4	cup parsley, chopped
1/2	pint oysters, finely chopped
16	fl. oz. Cajun Injector Beef Marinade (Creole Garlic recipe)

DUCK GUMBO

Serves 16 (approx.)

Inject ducks with beef marinade, cut into serving pieces and put the ducks to boil in water over medium heat. While ducks are boiling, make a roux in an iron skillet, by putting the oil and flour together. Cook over low heat, stirring constantly until the flour is a dark brown. Add onions, celery, and bell pepper, cooking until the vegetables are wilted. Add the roux to the boiling ducks and cook until the duck is tender, about 2 hours total. When the ducks are almost done, add parsley, green onions and oysters (optional), and cook for 30 minutes. Season to taste with Cajun Shake and add water, if necessary, for proper consistency. Serve hot with cooked rice.

NUTRITION INFORMATION PER SERVING*

Calories	Saturated Fat	Total Fat	Protein	Carbohydrates	Cholesterol	Sodium
726.5	69.5g	20g	5g	5g	129mg	124mg

*Nutritional information does not reflect rice.

SHRIMP

Cajun Sidebar:

A traditional Louisiana dish, Jambalaya is adaptable using any seafood, chicken or sausage. Serve as a side dish or a main course with salad.

FRONT PORCH SHRIMP & SAUSAGE JAMBALAYA

INGREDIENTS	
1	lb. sausage (smoked pork) sliced thin
1	tbsp. olive oil
2/3	cup chopped green bell pepper
2	cloves garlic
3/4	cup chopped fresh parsley
1	cup chopped celery
2	16 oz. cans tomatoes
2	cups chicken broth
1	cup chopped green onions
1	tbsp. Cajun Shake
1/2	tsp. salt
1/4	tsp. black pepper
1/4	tsp. cayenne pepper
2	cups washed long grain rice
3	lbs. raw shrimp

Serves 10

In a 4 quart heavy pot, sauté sausage; remove with slotted spoon. Add oil to drippings and sauté green pepper, garlic, parsley and celery 5 minutes. Chop tomatoes and reserve liquid. Add tomatoes with liquid, broth and onions. Stir in spices. Add rice which has been washed and rinsed three times. Add sausage and cook 30 minutes, covered, over low heat, stirring occasionally. After most liquid has been absorbed by rice, add shrimp and cook until pink. After turning off heat, let stand covered for several minutes — then dish up and ENJOY!

NUTRITION INFORMATION PER SERVING

Calories	Saturated Fat	Total Fat	Protein	Carbohydrates	Cholesterol	Sodium
471	7g	22g	36g	32g	294mg	916mg

Cajun Sidebar:

This dish is like a "Cajun Stew." To take the tartness out of the tomatoes, add a pinch (1/8 tsp.) of sugar to this recipe.

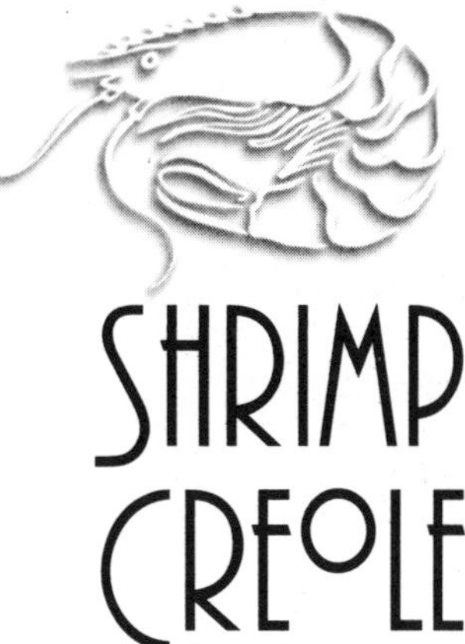

SHRIMP CREOLE

INGREDIENTS	
2 1/2	lbs. raw, unpeeled shrimp
1 1/2	tbsp. oil
1 1/2	tbsp. flour
1/3	cup finely chopped green bell peppers
1/2	cup chopped onions
1	stalk celery, chopped fine
8	oz. can tomato sauce
16	oz. can stewed tomatoes
1	clove garlic, minced
3	dashes Louisiana-style hot sauce
1/4	tsp. black pepper
1/4	tsp. cayenne pepper
2	tbsp. chopped fresh parsley
3/4	cup chopped green onion
2	cups cooked rice

Serves 6

Peel and devein shrimp.

In a large pot, heat oil and add flour, stirring constantly until roux is dark brown. Add onion, green pepper and celery; cook until tender. Pour in tomato sauce, tomatoes and 2 cups water. Blend well. Add garlic, hot sauce, a pinch of sugar (optional), salt and peppers. Simmer 30 minutes, stirring occasionally. Add shrimp, parsley and green onions. Cook 30 minutes. Serve over rice.

NUTRITION INFORMATION PER SERVING

Calories	Saturated Fat	Total Fat	Protein	Carbohydrates	Cholesterol	Sodium
474	1g	6g	45g	59g	369mg	435mg

Cajun Sidebar:

When you're in a hurry, but still want that great New Orleans barbeque shrimp taste, try this recipe. Creole Garlic marinade makes this meal a snap to put together.

INGREDIENTS

☞	**Cajun Injector Creole Garlic Marinade**
1/2	**fresh lemon**
1/2	**stick butter**
2	**dozen jumbo shrimp in shells**

RON'S BAR-B-QUE SHRIMP

Serves 2

Wash shrimp thoroughly. Pinch off portion of head from the eyes forward. Melt butter in a large skillet. Place shrimp in a single layer in the butter. Shake marinade well and pour over shrimp until almost covered. Cover the top with black pepper.

Cook for 5 minutes, occasionally shaking skillet in a back and forth motion – *do not stir.* Just before removing shrimp from heat, squeeze 1/2 fresh lemon on top of shrimp and sauce. Remove from heat, serve immediately in bowls with hot french bread on the side. *If you don't "sop" your bread in the sauce, it's your mistake!*

P.S. (For an extra treat — try using ***Cajun Injector Red Wine Marinade.*** *Umm Umm Good!)*

NUTRITION INFORMATION PER SERVING

Calories	Saturated Fat	Total Fat	Protein	Carbohydrates	Cholesterol	Sodium
93	0g	2g	17g	2g	128mg	Varies

Cajun Sidebar:

Stuffed shrimp are great as a meal on their own or try combining them with other fried seafoods for a special seafood platter.

TIP:

AFTER SPLITTING THE LARGE SHRIMP DOWN THE BACK, PRIOR TO FILLING, PLACE ON LIGHTLY GREASED COOKIE SHEET AND FILL WITH STUFFING. COVER WITH PLASTIC WRAP AND FREEZE. WHEN FROZEN, COMBINE ONE MEAL'S WORTH OF SHRIMP IN FREEZER BAG

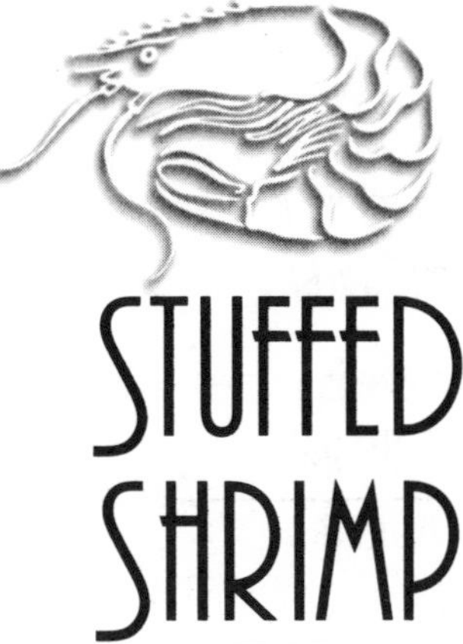

STUFFED SHRIMP

INGREDIENTS	
2	large onions, chopped
2	bell peppers, chopped
6	stalks celery, chopped
3	pods garlic, chopped
1/2	cup cooking oil
1	lb. raw shrimp, chopped
☞	Cajun Shake to taste
2	cups day-old bread
1	lb. lump crab meat
1	tbsp. parsley, chopped
2	eggs
4	lbs. large shrimp, whole

Serves 12

Saute onions, bell peppers, celery and garlic in oil until tender. Add chopped raw shrimp and Cajun Shake. Cook until the shrimp are done.

Toast the day old bread and soak in water to moisten. Squeeze out water and add the wet bread to the sauteed mixture, a little at a time, mixing well. Add crab meat and parsley and cook for 5 minutes. Set aside to cool. Add raw eggs while mixture is cooling.

Peel and devein large shrimp, leaving tail shell on. Split down the back with a sharp knife, making sure not to cut the shrimp completely through. Fill the backs of the shrimp with dressing then freeze.

When ready to cook, dip shrimp in flour, then in beaten egg and milk mixture, then in flour again. Fry in deep oil at 350 degrees until golden brown.

NUTRITION INFORMATION PER SERVING

Calories	Saturated Fat	Total Fat	Protein	Carbohydrates	Cholesterol	Sodium
275	2.4g	12.7g	36.4g	3.9g	313mg	490mg

Cajun Sidebar:

How to make a shrimp stock:

After peeling off shells and removing the shrimps' heads, place shells and heads in several quarts of seasoned water. Boil for 1 hour over low heat. Strain out shells and use in recipes or freeze. You can also add celery, onions and carrots when boiling the stock to deepen the flavor.

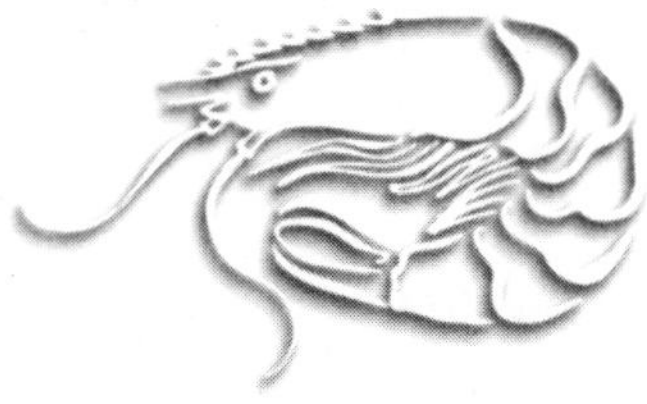

Garlic Shrimp Pasta

INGREDIENTS	
1/2	tsp. dried thyme
1/2	tsp. sweet paprika
1/2	tsp. ground cayenne pepper
3/4	tsp. salt
6	tbsp. unsalted butter
3/4	cup (including tops) chopped green onions
1	tbsp. minced garlic
1/2	tsp. white pepper
1/2	tsp. onion powder
1/4	tsp. finely ground black pepper
1/3	lb. angel hair pasta
16	large shrimp
3/4	cup homemade shrimp stock

Serves 2

Peel and devein shrimp, using shrimp heads to make 3/4 cups stock (see sidebar). Cook pasta and set aside.

Melt 6 tbsp. butter in large skillet. Add shrimp, seasonings and green onions. Cook until shrimp turn pink, approximately 1 minute.

Add shrimp stock, shaking skillet in a back and forth motion (do not stir — keeps sauce from separating). Cook another minute.

Add cooked pasta to shrimp mixture folding over and over until heated through and through.

Serve on warm plate. Add salad, french bread and VOILA! You have a great dinner.

NUTRITION INFORMATION PER SERVING

Calories	Saturated Fat	Total Fat	Protein	Carbohydrates	Cholesterol	Sodium
797	23g	42g	58g	47g	500mg	1252mg

Cajun Sidebar:

Jambalaya can also be made with sausage and chicken. Use the basic recipe and substitute for shrimp, or add with the shrimp.

DIANE'S SHRIMP JAMBALAYA

INGREDIENTS	
1	16 oz. pkg. bacon
1	large onion
2	stalks celery
1	small green bell pepper
4	green onions
2	cups rice
3	cups water
1	tsp. kitchen bouquet
2	lbs. shrimp
1	8 oz. can tomato sauce
1	10 oz. can Rotel tomatoes

Serves 8

Cut bacon in small pieces and fry in large pot. Remove bacon and set aside.

Sauté all vegetables in bacon drippings except green onions. Add water, tomato sauce, Rotel tomatoes, kitchen bouquet and shrimp. Bring to boil, then add rice. Cover and cook on medium heat for 20 minutes. Turn off heat, then add bacon and green onions.

NUTRITION INFORMATION PER SERVING

Calories	Saturated Fat	Total Fat	Protein	Carbohydrates	Cholesterol	Sodium
625	12.5g	34.3g	33g	46.1g	259mg	992mg

FISH & SEAFOOD

Cajun Sidebar:

If catfish is unavailable, try fresh trout or a whitefish from your region.

PECAN CATFISH

INGREDIENTS	
5	catfish fillets, 5-7 oz. each
1	cup flour
2	eggs
1/2	cup milk
3	oz. unsalted butter
2	cups roasted pecans, chopped
1	tsp. Cajun Injector Beef Marinade (Creole Garlic recipe)
☞	juice of one lemon
☞	salt and pepper to taste

Serves 5

Season catfish with salt and pepper. Dredge in flour, then dip in egg wash made with beaten eggs and milk. Dredge in flour again.

After dredging, pan fry in melted butter.

Puree 1-1/2 cups pecans, butter, lemon juice and marinade. Spread over catfish.

Garnish with pecans and serve.

NUTRITION INFORMATION PER SERVING						
Calories	Saturated Fat	Total Fat	Protein	Carbohydrates	Cholesterol	Sodium
756	14g	55g	38g	28g	217mg	143mg

Cajun Sidebar:

Try to buy the tuna steaks fresh instead of frozen. To really get the most flavor, wrap tuna steaks in plastic wrap and inject with the marinade. Discard plastic wrap and grill.

GRILLED TUNA

INGREDIENTS	
6	Tuna Steaks
8	oz. Cajun Injector Creole Garlic recipe
1/2	stick butter

Serves 6

Slice at home or have your seafood market slice fresh tuna into 1 to 1 1/2 inch steaks.

Melt butter, mix with marinade. Add enough marinade to cover steaks. Marinate about 15 minutes.

Place steaks on grill and continue to brush marinade on steaks as they cook.

It doesn't come any better than this!

NUTRITION INFORMATION PER SERVING

Calories	Saturated Fat	Total Fat	Protein	Carbohydrates	Cholesterol	Sodium
70	4.8g	7.7g	0.1g	0.0g	21mg	78mg

Cajun Sidebar:

For an even more elegant presentation, add cooked shrimp, crab-meat or crawfish tails to the lemon sauce before pouring over the filets.

INGREDIENTS	
6	Trout Filets
1	cup milk
1	tsp. salt
1/4	tsp. black pepper
1/2	cup sifted flour
1/4	cup butter
1/2	cup slivered almonds

TROUT ALMANDINE

Serves 6

Salt and pepper trout. Dip in milk, then roll in flour, making sure that the entire filet is well coated. Melt butter in skillet and sauté filets, browning evenly on both sides (about 5 or 10 minutes or until golden brown). Remove trout to warm platter. In same skillet, add slivered almonds and sauté until light brown. Squeeze a little fresh lemon juice in skillet after removing from heat. Pour over fish and serve while hot.

NUTRITION INFORMATION PER SERVING

Calories	Saturated Fat	Total Fat	Protein	Carbohydrates	Cholesterol	Sodium
207	6.2g	15.3g	4.9g	12.3g	26mg	495mg

Cajun Sidebar:

This recipe can also be done in the microwave. Cover fish with plastic wrap. Poke holes in wrap to vent. Microwave on high for 5 minutes. Turn dish. Microwave again until filets flake with fork.

Baked Catfish Divine

INGREDIENTS	
6	catfish filets (3-4 oz. ea.)
1	stick butter
1	whole, fresh lemon
☞	fresh parsley, chopped
☞	Cajun Shake

Serves 6

Coat the bottom of an oven proof pan with butter. Place catfish filets in pan, pour melted butter over fish. Sprinkle each filet with Cajun Shake and the chopped parsley.

Bake in a 400 degree oven until the fish is done, about 20 minutes. When you remove the fish from the oven, sprinkle it liberally with lemon juice. Serve immediately.

To lower calories & fat, use Cajun Injector Poultry marinade instead of butter. Tastes wonderful — you won't miss the calories.

NUTRITION INFORMATION PER SERVING

Calories	Saturated Fat	Total Fat	Protein	Carbohydrates	Cholesterol	Sodium
318	11.1g	22.1g	29g	0.9g	133mg	256mg

Cajun Sidebar:

If red snapper is unavailable, you can substitute any regionally available fresh fish.

INGREDIENTS	
4	lbs. red snapper
1	pint oysters
2	lbs. raw shrimp
1	4 oz can mushrooms
1/4	cup sherry wine
2	tbsp. chopped parsley
1	whole lemon, sliced

RED SNAPPER COURTBOUILLON (KOO-B-YON)

Serves 15

Place filets in large dish.

Sprinkle oysters, shrimp and mushrooms over fish.

Cover with "Creole Sauce" (see page 83 for recipe).

Sprinkle with wine, lemon slices and parsley. Bake 25 minutes at 350 degrees.

Serve over rice.

NUTRITION INFORMATION PER SERVING						
Calories	Saturated Fat	Total Fat	Protein	Carbohydrates	Cholesterol	Sodium
202	1g	3g	40g	2g	181mg	251mg

Cajun Sidebar:

Creole Sauce is a great addition to just about any grilled, fried or broiled fish.

INGREDIENTS

1/4	cup flour
1/4	cup oil or bacon drippings
2	cups chopped onions
1	cup chopped green bell peppers
1/4	cup chopped green onions including tops
2	cloves garlic
1	cup chopped celery with leaves
1	tsp. thyme
2	bay leaves
2	tsp. Cajun Shake
1/2	tsp. pepper
16 oz.	can stewed tomatoes
6 oz.	can tomato paste
8 oz.	can tomato sauce
1	tsp. Louisiana hot sauce
1/2	cup chopped parsley
1	tbsp. lemon juice
1/2	cup sherry wine

RED SNAPPER COURTBOUILLON (KOO-B-YON) "CREOLE SAUCE"

Serves 15

In large dutch oven make a dark roux using the flour and oil (or bacon drippings).

Add other ingredients, cooking about 5 minutes, and pour over red snapper, shrimp, oysters and mushrooms **(recipe on page 81)**. Bake 25 minutes at 350 degrees.

NUTRITION INFORMATION PER SERVING

Calories	Saturated Fat	Total Fat	Protein	Carbohydrates	Cholesterol	Sodium
77	0g	4g	1g	7g	0mg	89mg

Cajun Sidebar:

This soup is great as a meal. Serve with warm French bread and a salad.

Front Porch Bouillabaisse

INGREDIENTS	
1	cup chopped onions
1	cup chopped celery
1	cup chopped green bell peppers
1/2	cup olive oil, divided
3	cloves garlic, crushed
3	lbs. catfish filets, cut into small pieces
1	bunch parsley
1	16 oz. can tomatoes
2	cups dry white wine
1	cup water
☞	ground cayenne pepper
2	bay leaves
1	lb. raw shrimp, peeled
1	lb. white crab meat
12	oz. oysters w/liquid
☞	Cajun Shake to taste

Serves 20

Sauté the first 4 vegetables in 1/4 cup olive oil until tender. Lightly sauté the catfish (or any bland white fish) in the remaining olive oil. In a large pot, combine the vegetables and fish with all of the remaining ingredients, except the seafood. Bring to a boil and simmer gently for about 30 minutes. Adjust seasonings and add more wine if more liquid is needed. Add seafood and simmer until fish is cooked (about 10 minutes). To serve, replace parsley with fresh sprigs and top each serving with slices of french bread toasted with parmesan cheese.

NUTRITION INFORMATION PER SERVING

Calories	Saturated Fat	Total Fat	Protein	Carbohydrates	Cholesterol	Sodium
192	2g	9g	22g	3g	97mg	205mg

Cajun Sidebar:

Gumbo is truly a treat. Although it takes more preparation time, it is well worth it. Many people prefer to eat potato salad with their gumbo.

Jeanne's Louisiana Seafood Gumbo

Serves 12

INGREDIENTS	
1	cup vegetable oil
1 1/2	cups flour
2	whole, large yellow onions, chopped
4	stalks celery, chopped
1	cup parsley, chopped
4	quarts water or seafood stock
2	lbs. shrimp, peeled and deveined
1	lb. lump crabmeat or claw meat
12	oz. oysters (optional)
3	lbs. gumbo crabs
1	bunch green onions
1	10 oz. can stewed tomatoes

Make this one ahead of time — it's even better the next day!

Make a roux with oil and flour, cooking over medium heat in a heavy dutch oven (black iron pot is even better). Stir roux mixture constantly until dark brown. Do not burn.

Add yellow onions and stir 5 minutes. Add celery and stir another minute. Add stewed tomatoes and blend.

Add water or stock slowly to make a smooth mixture, seasoning with Cajun Shake to taste. Cook 30 minutes, adding more liquid if necessary. Break crabs in half and add along with shrimp and crabmeat. Cook 30 minutes. 15 minutes before serving, add chopped green onions, parsley and oysters with their juice.

Serve hot over rice.

NUTRITION INFORMATION PER SERVING

Calories	Saturated Fat	Total Fat	Protein	Carbohydrates	Cholesterol	Sodium
376	4g	22g	24g	20g	200mg	520mg

Cajun Sidebar:

For the diet-wise, you can substitute milk for the half & half and use reduced calorie mayonnaise.

Front Porch Seafood Casserole

INGREDIENTS	
1	lb. fresh, cooked shrimp
1	lb. fresh crab meat
1/2	small green bell pepper, chopped fine
1/2	cup chopped onions
1	4 oz. jar pimentos, chopped
1/2	cup chopped celery
1	6 oz. can button mushrooms
1	cup mayonnaise
1/2	tsp. salt
1	cup half & half
1/8	tsp. pepper
1	tsp. worcestershire sauce
1/2-1	cup raw rice, cooked

A delightful casserole. Served with a salad and hot garlic bread and you've got yourself a winner.

Serves 8
(you may get 10 servings out of this — but my family eats hearty)

Mix first 7 ingredients and set aside.

Mix next 6 ingredients then blend all together. Place in 2 quart buttered casserole. Sprinkle with bread crumbs and bake 30 minutes at 375 degrees.

Variation: 1 pound of any seafood or a combination of seafood may replace shrimp in recipe.

NUTRITION INFORMATION PER SERVING

Calories	Saturated Fat	Total Fat	Protein	Carbohydrates	Cholesterol	Sodium
342	5g	19g	24g	18g	155mg	562mg

Cajun Sidebar:

As a young married girl living in New Orleans, I found out that I couldn't even boil water. My husband's Aunt, Ceil Saxon, showed me how to make this recipe, and my husband was forever grateful. (We were blessed that my husband was a great cook!)

JB'S TUNA CASSEROLE

INGREDIENTS	
2	**6 oz. cans solid white tuna in water**
2	**14 oz. cans english peas, drained**
2	**cans condensed cream of mushroom soup**
2	**eggs**
☞	**cheddar cheese, grated**
☞	**Cajun Shake to taste**

Serves 8

Cook small package of egg noodles and drain. Set aside.

Mix together tuna (drained), english peas (drained), and cream of mushroom soup. Fold in egg noodles.

Separate egg yolks and whites. Set aside whites to be used later. Beat yolks until blended. Add enough grated cheese to make a cup. Fold into tuna mixture. Bake in 350 degree oven until cheese melts. Beat egg whites until stiff. After cheese melts in casserole, fold in egg whites and return to oven. Cook until egg whites brown.

NUTRITION INFORMATION PER SERVING

Calories	Saturated Fat	Total Fat	Protein	Carbohydrates	Cholesterol	Sodium
74	1g	2g	13g	0g	71mg	184mg

CRAWFISH

Cajun Sidebar:

Etouffee means "smothered" and is kind of like a Cajun Stew. If crawfish is unavailable, use any seafood that is in season. Try this recipe with shrimp, redfish or any seafood from your region.

INGREDIENTS	
1	stick butter
1	white onion, chopped fine
1	lb. crawfish tails, cleaned
1/4	cup flour
1-1 1/2	cups water or homemade seafood stock (pg. 66)
1/4	cup fresh parsley, chopped fine
1/2	cup green onions, chopped fine
1	stalk celery, chopped fine
1/2	green bell pepper, chopped fine
3	cloves garlic, chopped fine
1 1/2	tbsp. tomato paste
1/4	tsp. cayenne pepper
☞	Cajun Shake, to taste
2	cups cooked rice

CRAWFISH ETOUFFEE

Serves 8

In a large skillet, melt the margarine over moderate heat. Add flour and brown lightly. Add chopped vegetables (except green onions and parsley) and tomato paste to the roux. Blend well. Add crawfish tails and season to taste with Cajun Shake and cayenne pepper. Cook on medium heat. Slowly add the water and stir in well. Reduce the heat and cook for approximately 20 minutes. A few minutes before you are ready to serve, add the parsley and green onions. Adjust seasonings if necessary. Serve over steaming white rice. Serve hot. Serves 6 to 8.

NUTRITION INFORMATION PER SERVING

Calories	Saturated Fat	Total Fat	Protein	Carbohydrates	Cholesterol	Sodium
359	2g	12g	15g	46g	79mg	215mg

Cajun Sidebar:

You can make this recipe low-fat by substituting milk for the half & half, using low-fat cheese and replacing the noodles with "eggless" ones. If the sauce becomes too thin, increase the flour until you reach the right consistency.

Chef Williams' Crawfish Fettuccine

INGREDIENTS	
1 1/2	sticks butter
3	onions, chopped
4	green onions, chopped
3	stalks celery, chopped
1	tbsp. flour
1	tbsp. parsley
2	lbs. crawfish tails
1/2	lb. egg noodles
1/2	pint half & half
3	cloves garlic
1/2	lb. light processed cheese
1/2	can jalapeno relish

Serves 6

Sauté yellow onions, green onions, bell pepper and celery in butter. Add flour, parsley and crawfish tails (or shrimp). Cook for 15 minutes.

Cook egg noodles until tender — set aside.

To crawfish mixture, add 1/2 can jalapeno relish, half & half, garlic and processed cheese. Cook about 15 minutes.

Combine noodles and crawfish mixture, coating all noodles well. Pour into large casserole dish. Top with parmesan cheese and bake 15 to 20 minutes at 350 degrees.

NUTRITION INFORMATION PER SERVING

Calories	Saturated Fat	Total Fat	Protein	Carbohydrates	Cholesterol	Sodium
678	21g	36g	43g	44g	343mg	962mg

Cajun Sidebar:

Roux is shortening and flour cooked together until it reaches a dark nutty-brown color. It is important to cook roux over medium heat, stirring constantly to prevent burning. If the roux "smokes" and smells burnt, throw it out and try it again. You can store unused roux in refrigerator in a covered jar for several weeks.

Premade roux is also available at grocery stores.

FRONT PORCH CRAWFISH PIE

INGREDIENTS	
1	lb. crawfish tails
1/4	cup onions, chopped
1	clove elephant garlic, chopped
1	tbsp. chopped green bell peppers
1	tbsp. chopped green onions
1	tbsp. chopped fresh parsley
1/4	cup flour
1/3	cup shortening
☞	Cajun Shake to taste

Serves 8

First we make a roux.

Heat shortening, add flour, stir constantly, until dark brown, being careful not to burn. Add onion, garlic and crawfish. Mix well, then add 1 cup water. Cook 30 minutes. Add more water if necessary. Season to taste with Cajun Shake. Add chopped peppers, green onions, parsley and cook 10 minutes longer. Remove from fire and allow to cool.

Make double pie crust from your favorite recipe. Line a 9 inch pie pan with one crust, fill with crawfish mixture and cover with remaining crust. Cut small slits in top of crust.

Bake at 350 degrees until brown and crisp.

Add your favorite salad and you have a great dinner for your family or friends.

NUTRITION INFORMATION PER SERVING*

Calories	Saturated Fat	Total Fat	Protein	Carbohydrates	Cholesterol	Sodium
166	1.6g	10.3g	14.2g	4.2g	101mg	39mg

*Nutritional information does not reflect pie crust

Cajun Sidebar:

This recipe makes a great hot dip for parties served with crackers or chips. It can also be an entree served over freshly cooked pasta — it's simply wonderful!

INGREDIENTS	
1	lb. crawfish tails
1/2	cup margarine
1	bunch green onions with tops, chopped
1/2	cup parsley, chopped
3	tbsp. flour
1	pint half & half
3	tbsp. sherry (optional)
☞	salt & red pepper to taste

Moi's Crawfish Elegante

Serves 6

In a skillet, sauté the crawfish in 1/4 cup of the margarine for 10 minutes. In another skillet, sauté the green onions and parsley in the remaining margarine and blend in the flour. Gradually add the cream, stirring constantly to make a thick sauce. Add the sherry (optional), crawfish, salt and red pepper. Blend well.

NUTRITION INFORMATION PER SERVING

Calories	Saturated Fat	Total Fat	Protein	Carbohydrates	Cholesterol	Sodium
437	15.2g	36.2g	21.0g	6.8g	204mg	267mg

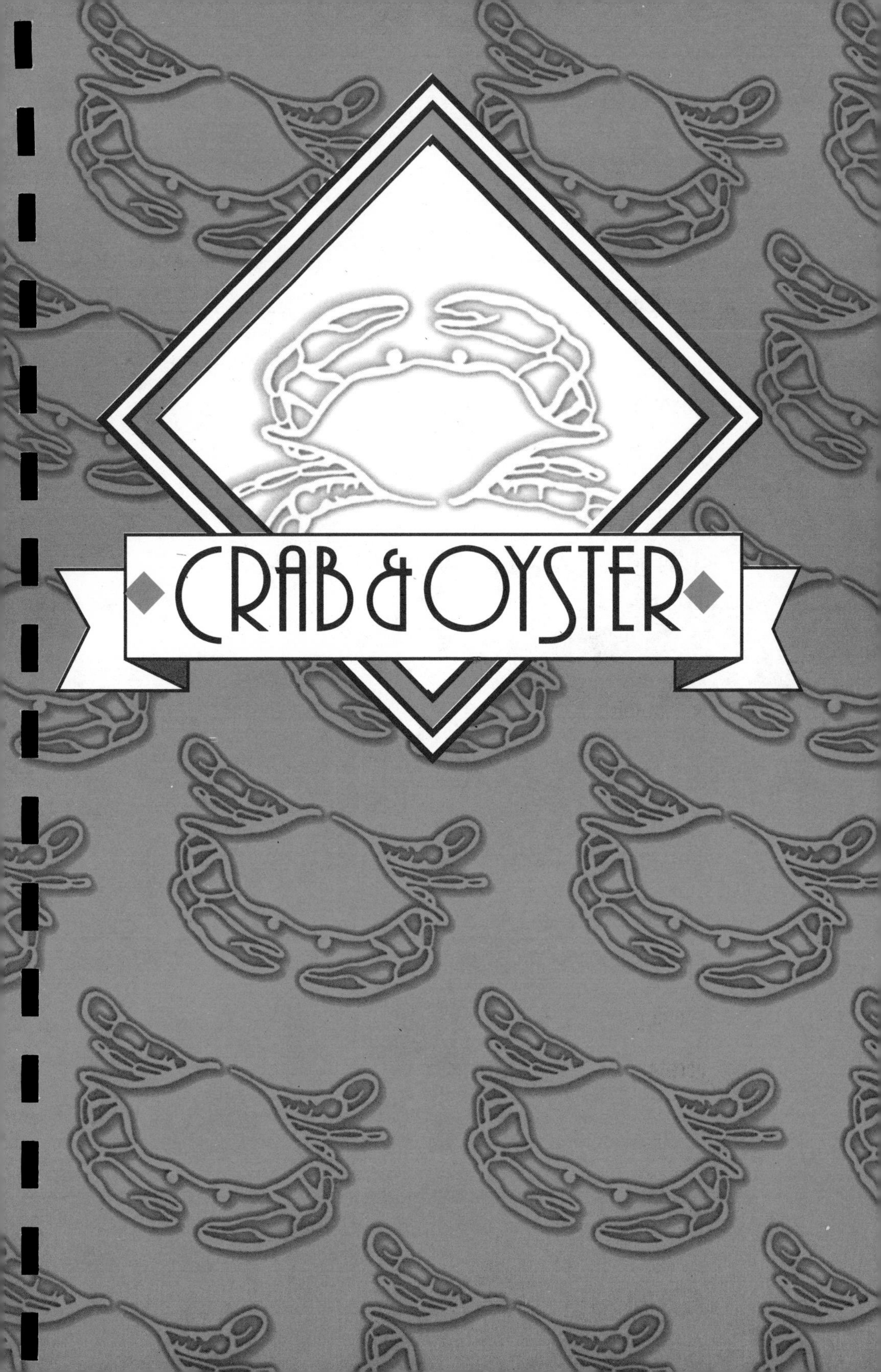
CRAB & OYSTER

Cajun Sidebar:

This recipe works well as a main entree or an appetizer. It can also be used to top fresh broiled or grilled fish

If you like this as much as we do, you might want to allow more than 1/4 pound of crabmeat per person.

ALINE'S LUMP CRABMEAT SAUTE

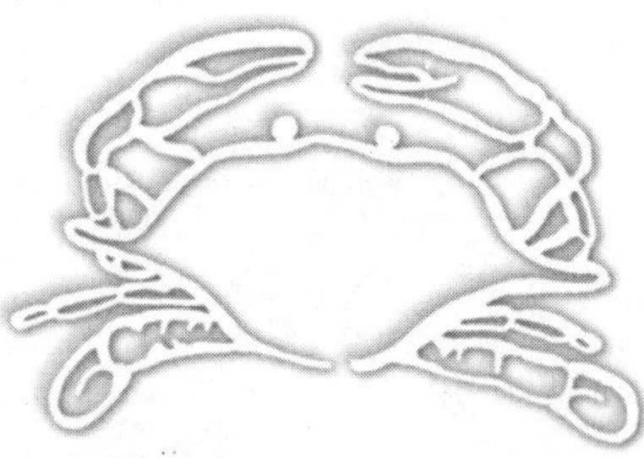

INGREDIENTS	
1	**lb. lump crabmeat**
1/2	**lb. butter**
☞	**fresh lemon juice**
☞	**green onion, finely chopped**

Serves 4

Use approximately 1/4 lb. lump crabmeat for each serving. In skillet, sauté until heated well, but do not brown. Sprinkle with fresh lemon juice.

Place in individual casseroles, sprinkle finely chopped green onions on top and serve.

NUTRITION INFORMATION PER SERVING

Calories	Saturated Fat	Total Fat	Protein	Carbohydrates	Cholesterol	Sodium
577	33.2g	54.6g	17g	4.5g	283mg	1294mg

Cajun Sidebar:

Definitely a southern favorite, and one of our customers' favorites. Serve with toasted garlic French bread and a salad for a complete meal.

Jeanne's Front Porch Crabmeat Au Gratin

INGREDIENTS

13	oz. evaporated milk
2	egg yolks
1	stalk celery, chopped
1/4	lb. butter
1/2	cup all-purpose flour
1	tsp. salt
1/2	tsp. ground red pepper
1/4	tsp. black pepper
1	lb. lump crabmeat
1/2	lb. cheddar cheese

Serves 6

Sauté onions and celery in oleo or butter until onions are wilted. Blend flour in well with this mixture. Pour in the milk gradually, stirring constantly. Add egg yolks, salt, red and black pepper; cook for 5 minutes.

Put crabmeat in a mixing bowl and pour the cooked sauce over the crabmeat. Blend well, folding over and over to keep lump crabmeat from breaking up.

Transfer into a lightly greased casserole and sprinkle with grated cheddar cheese. Bake at 375 degrees for 10 to 15 minutes or until light brown.

NUTRITION INFORMATION PER SERVING

Calories	Saturated Fat	Total Fat	Protein	Carbohydrates	Cholesterol	Sodium
532	23.4g	38.4g	26.3g	20.3g	205mg	1409mg

Cajun Sidebar:

I named this recipe after the lady who requested it for a catered luncheon held at the Front Porch almost 20 years ago. Although it was the first time I had prepared this recipe, it was such hit that I continued to serve it often as an entree or appetizer. I've even presented this as a spread for gourmet crackers.

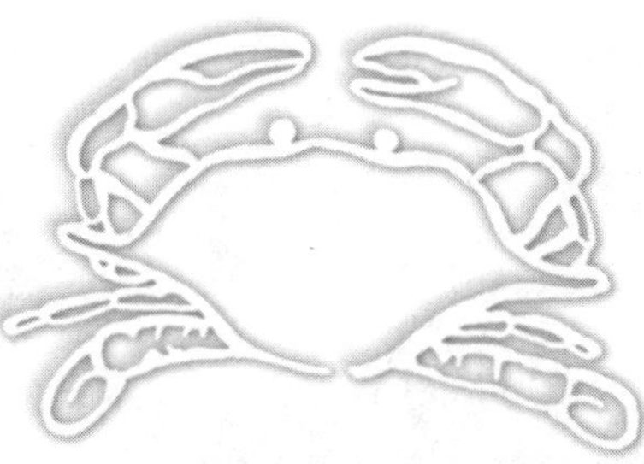

CRABMEAT IMPERIAL A LA CARMEN

INGREDIENTS	
1	whole green pepper, finely diced
2	whole pimientos, finely diced
1	tbsp. English mustard
1/2	tsp. white pepper
1	tsp. salt
2	whole beaten eggs
1	cup mayonnaise
3	lbs. lump crabmeat

Serves 8

Mix pepper and pimientos, add mustard, salt, pepper, eggs and mayonnaise. Mix well.

Add crabmeat, mixing with fingers so lumps are not broken. Divide mixture into 8 crab shells or ramekins, heaping them lightly. Top with a little mayonnaise and sprinkle with a little paprika. Bake at 350 degrees for 15 minutes.

NUTRITION INFORMATION PER SERVING

Calories	Saturated Fat	Total Fat	Protein	Carbohydrates	Cholesterol	Sodium
413	9g	29g	27g	12g	291mg	1677mg

Cajun Sidebar:

These recipes are great on a cold winter's night. Try serving with crackers floating on top.

To cut fat in Corn & Crab Soup, substitute evaporated skim milk in place of half & half.

To make oyster stew really rich, use 1/2 half & half and 1/2 milk.

J.B. Corn & Crab Soup

Serves 8

INGREDIENTS	
1	lb. lump crabmeat
1	onion, chopped
2	stalks celery, chopped fine
1	bunch green onions, chopped
1	16 oz. can cream style corn
2	pints half & half
1	stick butter
☞	Cajun Shake to taste

Sauté onions, green onions and celery in butter until onions are clear. DO NOT BROWN. Add corn and simmer about 10 minutes. Slowly add half & half and mix well. Add crabmeat and seasonings, continue to simmer apprx. 10 minutes. Serve and stand back for compliments.

NUTRITION INFORMATION PER SERVING

Calories	Saturated Fat	Total Fat	Protein	Carbohydrates	Cholesterol	Sodium
381	16g	26g	16g	20g	109mg	348mg

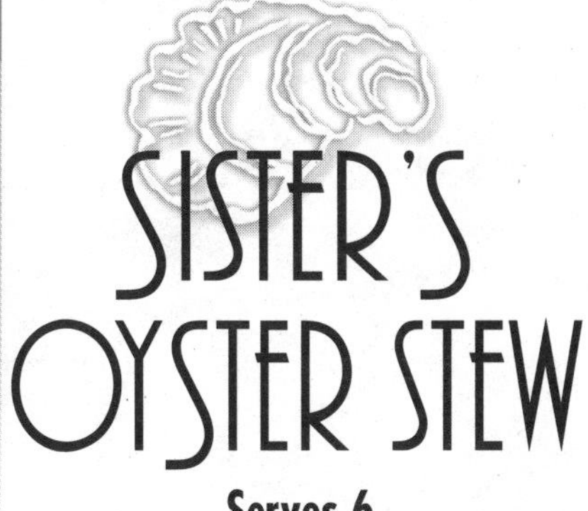

Sister's Oyster Stew

Serves 6

INGREDIENTS	
$1^1/_2$	sticks butter
$1^1/_2$	quarts milk
1	pint oysters
☞	fresh parsley, chopped (optional)
☞	green onions, chopped

Melt butter in a 3 quart pan. Add milk and oysters. Bring stew almost to a boil, being careful not to scald milk. Add chopped parsley, green onions, and a dash or two of hot sauce.

NUTRITION INFORMATION PER SERVING

Calories	Saturated Fat	Total Fat	Protein	Carbohydrates	Cholesterol	Sodium
414	20g	33g	14g	15g	141mg	446mg

Cajun Sidebar:

This was a popular appetizer at the Front Porch Restaurant. We preferred using the small to medium sized oysters.

Front Porch Baked Oysters

INGREDIENTS	
3	tsp. fresh lemon juice
$1^1/_2$	tsp. Louisiana-style hot sauce
6	slices bacon, crisp fried & crumbled
12	thin slices Wisconsin jalapeno jack cheese
12	oysters, on the half shell
3	tsp. Cajun Injector Beef Marinade (Creole Garlic recipe)

Serves 2

Preheat oven to broil.

Prepare two large pie pans filled with rock salt.

Open oysters and place 6 shell halves on each pie pan. Loosen oysters from shell. Sprinkle 1/4 tsp. of lemon juice and 3 tsp. of Creole Garlic recipe on each oyster. Sprinkle 1/8 tsp. of hot sauce on each oyster. Top each oyster with 1/2 slice of crumbled bacon and a slice of jalapeno cheese.

Run the oysters under the broiler until the cheese melts. Serve at once.

NUTRITION INFORMATION PER SERVING

Calories	Saturated Fat	Total Fat	Protein	Carbohydrates	Cholesterol	Sodium
386	14.8g	39.9g	6g	0.9g	47mg	510mg

Cajun Sidebar:

These are great for a party. Prepare in advance and freeze until needed.

INGREDIENTS	
4	dozen oysters with liquid
1	tbsp. butter
1	tbsp. flour
2	tbsp. minced fresh parsley
1	small onion, finely chopped
1	cup mushroom stems & pieces, chopped
1/4	tsp. fresh lemon juice
12	patty shells

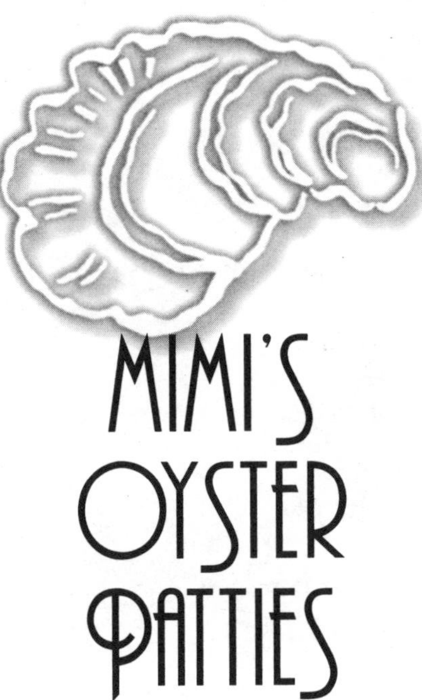

MIMI'S OYSTER PATTIES

Great as appetizers for parties or as a meal!

Serves 12

Bring oysters and liquid to a boil, then simmer until edges begin to curl. Melt butter in skillet over medium heat. Add onion and blend in flour until smooth. Add 1/2 cup mushroom juice, salt, pepper (to taste) and mushrooms. Mix. Add oysters and lemon juice. Cook 5 minutes. Pour into patty shells. Bake at 425 degrees for 15 minutes.

NUTRITION INFORMATION PER SERVING

Calories	Saturated Fat	Total Fat	Protein	Carbohydrates	Cholesterol	Sodium
22	1.2g	2g	0.2g	0.8g	5mg	20mg

*Nutritional information does not reflect patty shells.

Cajun Sidebar:

Cutting back on the amount of water turns this recipe into a great hot dip.

Oyster Bayou Spaghetti

INGREDIENTS

1/2	**cup fresh parsley**
1/4	**cup flour**
1	**cup green onions with tops, chopped**
1	**stick butter**
1	**quart oyster water**
24	**small oysters**
1/2	**oz. Cajun Injector Beef Marinade (Creole Garlic recipe)**
1	**lb. thin spaghetti, cooked**

Serves 4

Melt butter. Blend in flour and cook until foam appears — DO NOT BROWN.

Boil oysters in oyster water until edges of oysters curl. If you do not have enough oyster water to make four cups, add water. Remove oysters and set aside, add boiling water from oysters to the flour and stir rapidly over medium heat. Cook ten minutes.

Add parsley and green onions, marinade, and salt and pepper to taste. Cook 15 minutes over a low fire.

Cook spaghetti. Drop oysters into sauce, and dish sauce over spaghetti.

NUTRITION INFORMATION PER SERVING*

Calories	Saturated Fat	Total Fat	Protein	Carbohydrates	Cholesterol	Sodium
406	14.4g	23.9g	7.1g	40.5g	62mg	390mg

VEGETABLE ENTREES

Cajun Sidebar:

A very exciting version of the southern "smothered" cabbage.

INGREDIENTS	
1	head cabbage
1	bunch carrots
1	bag turkey or pork "Tasso")
1/2	lb. bacon
1	onion, purple
1	onion, yellow
1/4	cup sugar
2	tbsp. Cajun Injector Beef Marinade (Creole Garlic recipe)

Uncle Paul's Cabbage

"Tasso" is a highly seasoned Cajun smoked ham or turkey.

Serves 6

Fry bacon crisp, remove from skillet and sauté onions in bacon drippings.

Cube "Tasso," boil in water for 15 minutes. Add carrots and cabbage to "Tasso" water and bring to a boil.

Add seasonings and bacon back to cabbage mixture. Reduce heat to a good simmer and cook until cabbage is tender.

NUTRITION INFORMATION PER SERVING

Calories	Saturated Fat	Total Fat	Protein	Carbohydrates	Cholesterol	Sodium
317	8g	22g	6g	23g	25mg	316mg

Cajun Sidebar:

Cabbage rolls are a great way to make leftover meat a new meal. Try chicken, pork or lamb ground up in place of beef.

TIP:

FOR A DIFFERENT TASTE AND NO ADDED CALORIES, SHAKE CAJUN INJECTOR MARINADE ORIGINAL RECIPE FOR BEEF ON BAKED POTATOES — YOU'LL NEVER MISS THE BUTTER!

INGREDIENTS	
1	head cabbage
1	lb. ground round
1	stick butter
3/4	cups raw rice
16	oz. tomato sauce
2	tsp. Cajun Shake
2	cloves minced garlic
☞	cinnamon to taste

Mary's Cabbage Rolls

Serves 6

Separate cabbage leaves and trim off the stem. Drop into boiling water and remove immediately. Set leaves aside.

Filling: combine ground round (raw), melted butter, raw rice, 1 cup tomato sauce, Cajun Shake, garlic and cinnamon in large mixing bowl. Fill each cabbage leaf with 1 tbsp. of filling and roll the leaves away from you. Place the cabbage rolls into a heavy pot, arranging the rolls close to each other. Add enough hot water to cover the cabbage rolls. Add remaining tomato sauce seasoned with garlic and cinnamon and pour over cabbage rolls. Cover and bring to boil. Reduce heat and let simmer for 15 more minutes (making sure rice is cooked) with cover on. Enjoy!

NUTRITION INFORMATION PER SERVING

Calories	Saturated Fat	Total Fat	Protein	Carbohydrates	Cholesterol	Sodium
268	10g	16g	4g	28g	41mg	184mg

Cajun Sidebar:

Creole stuffed tomatoes can be used as a side dish or main entree. I like to serve a Caesar salad along with it to balance out the meal.

CREOLE STUFFED TOMATOES

INGREDIENTS	
8	fresh tomatoes
1	cup onions, chopped
3/4	cup green bell peppers, chopped
1/2	tsp. fresh garlic cloves, crushed
1	tsp. thyme leaves, crushed
1/2	cup uncooked instant rice
12	oz. ground pork sausage
☞	Cajun Shake to taste

Serves 4

Preheat oven to 400 degrees. Use tomatoes held at room temperature until fully ripe. Cut a thin slice from the top of each tomato; scoop out and reserve pulp leaving 1/4 inch thick shells; set shells aside. Chop pulp (makes about 2-1/2 cups); set aside. In a large skillet, cook sausage until still pink in the center, about 3 minutes. Add onion, green pepper and garlic. Cook and stir until sausage is brown and vegetables tender, about 4 minutes. Add reserved tomato pulp, thyme, and Cajun Shake seasoning to taste. Boil uncovered until tomatoes are softened and slightly thickened, about 3 minutes. Stir in rice. Place tomato shells in a 12x8x2 inch pan. Divide sausage mixture evenly among tomato shells. Bake, uncovered, until rice is cooked and filling hot, about 15 minutes

NUTRITION INFORMATION PER SERVING

Calories	Saturated Fat	Total Fat	Protein	Carbohydrates	Cholesterol	Sodium
386	14.8g	39.9g	6g	0.9g	47mg	510mg

Cajun Sidebar:

The secret to this recipe is to boil the peppers until they are almost falling apart. This recipe is my family's favorite.

Early in my marriage,my aunt, Emma Gormley, taught me this recipe (the New Orleans City Park Tad Gormley Stadium is named after her husband). She was an excellent cook and loved to entertain — maybe a little bit rubbed off on me.

CREOLE STUFFED BELL PEPPERS

INGREDIENTS	
3	whole green bell peppers
1 1/2	lbs. ground round
1	cup cooked rice
10	oz. tomato soup
2	tbsp. minced garlic
☞	Cajun Shake

Serves 6

Wash, halve and core bell peppers. Cook in salted water until very tender.

Mix ground round, rice, garlic and Cajun Shake together. Add 1/2 can soup. Mix well with hands.

Place bell peppers in ungreased casserole. Fill each pepper with ground round mixture.

Add 1/2 can water to rest of soup and mix well. Pour over stuffed peppers.

Cook at 350 degrees for approximately 45 minutes or until done.

NUTRITION INFORMATION PER SERVING

Calories	Saturated Fat	Total Fat	Protein	Carbohydrates	Cholesterol	Sodium
390	9.6g	24.3g	22.3g	20.4g	85mg	408mg

Cajun Sidebar:

I bet even the most timid will like eating green vegetables after they have tried this recipe. You will use this casserole time and time again.

PEAS & ASPARAGUS CASSEROLE

Quick and simple, but it will draw raves from everyone!

INGREDIENTS

2	16 oz. cans petite peas, drained
2	16 oz. cans asparagus, drained
2	10oz. cans cream of mushroom soup
1/4	stick butter, cut into dots
1/2	cup grated cheese

Serves 10

Preheat oven to 350 degrees. Mix peas, asparagus and soup together in a buttered casserole (shallow 3 quart). Cajun Shake to taste. Dot with the butter and sprinkle grated cheese on top. Bake at 350 degrees until the casserole is bubbling, approximately 30 minutes. Serve hot.

NUTRITION INFORMATION PER SERVING

Calories	Saturated Fat	Total Fat	Protein	Carbohydrates	Cholesterol	Sodium
199	3.8g	8.9g	10.9g	18.9g	13mg	727mg

SIDES & SALADS

Cajun Sidebar:

The trick to this salad is to let it marinate in its own seasonings. Make the day before and allow it to chill overnight. Place on a bed of lettuce before serving.

TIP:

ADD CAJUN INJECTOR MARINADE ORIGINAL RECIPE FOR BEEF TO BLOODY MARY MIX FOR A GREAT SPICY DRINK.

West Indies Salad

INGREDIENTS	
1	lb. lump crabmeat
1	large onion, chopped
4	oz. cider vinegar
3	oz. salad oil
3	oz. ice water
☞	celery seed
☞	capers
☞	salt & pepper to taste
☞	bay leaves

Serves 4

Layer crabmeat and onion. Sprinkle with salt, pepper, celery seed and capers. Place a few bay leaves on top.

Add as many layers as you have crabmeat and onion. Stir vinegar, oil and water with a fork and pour over the crabmeat mixture. Cover and place in refrigerator for two or three hours. Improves with age. Let sit at least overnight before serving. Easily increased.

NUTRITION INFORMATION PER SERVING

Calories	Saturated Fat	Total Fat	Protein	Carbohydrates	Cholesterol	Sodium
391	7.3g	30.1g	17.5g	12.7g	159mg	830mg

Cajun Sidebar:

Simple and quick to prepare, this dish is great as a side to beef and pork entrees.

If you cannot find a Vidalia onion, you can substitute a whole yellow onion.

Baked Vidalia Onion

INGREDIENTS	
1	**large, whole Vidalia onion**
2	**tbsp. margarine or butter**
1	**tbsp. Cajun Shake**

Serves 2

Peel whole Vidalia onion. Cut 8 slices into onion being careful not to cut all the way through. Place in microwave-safe dish.

Sprinkle on Cajun Shake, making sure to get Cajun Shake inside each slice that you made in the onion.

Top with 2 tbsp. margarine or butter. Cover with plastic wrap. Punch a couple of holes into the plastic to let steam escape.

Microwave on high 5-8 minutes or until onion is done.

NUTRITION INFORMATION PER SERVING

Calories	Saturated Fat	Total Fat	Protein	Carbohydrates	Cholesterol	Sodium
165	2g	11.7g	1.9g	13.1g	0mg	138mg

Cajun Sidebar:

I really like serving baked garlic along with baked brie, apples and French bread as an appetizer or a light supper.

INGREDIENTS	
8	fresh garlic bulbs
2-4	tbsp. olive oil
4	rosemary sprigs or oregano sprigs

HERB ROASTED GARLIC

Serves 8

Remove outer layers of skin from garlic, leaving cloves and head intact. Place all heads on double thickness of foil; top with olive oil and herbs. Fold up and seal. Bake in 375 degree oven for about 1 hour. Serve one whole head per person. Squeeze cooked cloves from skin onto cooked meat and vegetables or on French or rye bread.

Note: if you prefer, you may trim tops off garlic heads to expose tops of garlic cloves. This makes cloves easier to scoop out. Then bake as instructed. Cooking time may be slightly reduced.

NUTRITION INFORMATION PER SERVING

Calories	Saturated Fat	Total Fat	Protein	Carbohydrates	Cholesterol	Sodium
37	0.5g	3.5g	0.2g	1.3g	0mg	1mg

Cajun Sidebar:

To get the optimum flavor from this recipe, use fresh corn. If it is not available, frozen corn is your next best bet.

AUNT JUNE'S COUNTRY CREAM CORN

INGREDIENTS	
2	quarts fresh corn
2 1/2	cups milk
1	stick margarine
3	tbsp. flour
3/4	cup sugar
2 1/2	tsp. salt
1/2	cup milk
1/2	tsp. black pepper

Serves 14

Use fresh corn that has been cut from cob.

In dutch oven combine margarine, 2-1/2 cups milk and corn. Bring to boil, stirring often to prevent sticking.

Combine plain flour, sugar and salt, mixing well until all lumps are gone. To this mix add 1/2 cup milk, stirring until smooth. Very slowly, add to corn mixture, stirring constantly to prevent sticking. Add black pepper to taste. Simmer uncovered for 20 minutes.

NUTRITION INFORMATION PER SERVING

Calories	Saturated Fat	Total Fat	Protein	Carbohydrates	Cholesterol	Sodium
251	2g	9g	5g	38g	7mg	525mg

Cajun Sidebar:

This holiday traditional recipe has been passed down through our family. This is especially good with pork.

INGREDIENTS	
1	stick butter
6	large whole sweet potatoes, fresh
2	tsp. vanilla
4	cups sugar
☞	enough water to cover

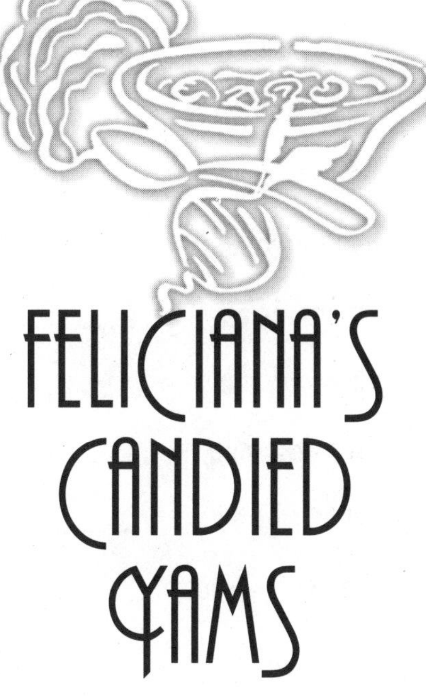

FELICIANA'S CANDIED YAMS

Serves 6

Peel and slice potatoes and place in sauce pan. Cover barely with water sugar. Boil until potatoes are tender and sauce has thickened. Add butter and vanilla. Serve.

NUTRITION INFORMATION PER SERVING						
Calories	Saturated Fat	Total Fat	Protein	Carbohydrates	Cholesterol	Sodium
412	10g	16g	2g	65g	41mg	173mg

Cajun Sidebar:

Cheese Balls are great to serve with salads and soups. As an appetizer, they never last long, so be sure to make enough to go around!

INGREDIENTS	
4	cups dry biscuit mix
10	oz. sharp cheddar cheese
1	lb. hot sausage

"FAIS DO DO"* CHEESE SAUSAGE BALLS

*Pronounced "Faye-Dough-Dough"

Makes Approximately 50 Balls

Grate cheese and let come to room temperature. Let sausage come to room temperature then mix all ingredients together until well mixed. Form into small balls, place on ungreased cookie sheet and put into 350 degree oven for 15-20 minutes.

You may make them up ahead of time and freeze them, taking out as many as you need. Makes a great appetizer.

NUTRITION INFORMATION PER SERVING

Calories	Saturated Fat	Total Fat	Protein	Carbohydrates	Cholesterol	Sodium
90	2g	4g	3g	11g	6mg	243mg

Cajun Sidebar:

This dish compliments pork, chicken, barbeque, or is great by itself.

INGREDIENTS	
1	pkg. spaghetti
1 1/2	sticks margarine
	enough milk to cover
6	boiled eggs

"WORMS" (REDNECK FETTUCCINE)

Not a very appetizing name — but young and old alike love this one. My husband learned this one from his mother; our children gave it the name.

Serves 8

Cook spaghetti as directed on package. Drain and rinse with hot water. Add spaghetti and 1-1/2 sticks of margarine (or butter) in sauce pan, mixing well until margarine is totally melted.

Cut up eggs while still warm and add to mixture in sauce pan. Mixing well, add enough milk until spaghetti is barely covered. Cook on medium, stirring occasionally to prevent sticking. It will thicken at this point. Add salt and pepper to taste. Serve hot and sit back and enjoy the compliments.

NUTRITION INFORMATION PER SERVING

Calories	Saturated Fat	Total Fat	Protein	Carbohydrates	Cholesterol	Sodium
56	1g	4g	5g	1g	159mg	48mg

Cajun Sidebar:

Remoulade sauce is great for dipping any seafood into. You can also use it in place of plain mayonnaise in tuna or shrimp salad.

REMOULADE SAUCE

This was my husband's favorite!

INGREDIENTS	
1	bunch green onions
1	stalk celery
3	tbsp. chopped parsley
3	cloves garlic
4	tbsp. creole mustard
2	tbsp. paprika
1/3	cup vinegar
2/3	cup olive oil

Serves 4

Grind onions, celery, garlic and parsley through a food grinder or blender. Add paprika, mustard, salt and pepper. Stir. Pour vinegar and mix thoroughly. Add olive oil, a small amount at a time. Stir and chill. This will keep in the refrigerat or for several weeks if tightly sealed

Boil, peel and devein shrimp. Place on bed of crisp lettuce and top with remoulade sauce.

NUTRITION INFORMATION PER SERVING

Calories	Saturated Fat	Total Fat	Protein	Carbohydrates	Cholesterol	Sodium
363	5g	38g	2g	5g	0mg	223mg

Cajun Sidebar:

This sauce can also be combined with potatoes left over from a crawfish boil. Great when left to sit overnight to allow all of the ingredients to blend well.

INGREDIENTS	
3	tbsp. horseradish
3	cloves garlic, chopped
1/2	cup creole mustard
1	small onion, chopped
4	celery leaves, chopped
2	tbsp. paprika
3	sprigs parsley, chopped
1	cup oil
1	oz. Worcestershire sauce

Remoulade Sauce II

Serves 6

Combine all ingredients and serve over boiled shrimp on a bed of lettuce.

NUTRITION INFORMATION PER SERVING						
Calories	Saturated Fat	Total Fat	Protein	Carbohydrates	Cholesterol	Sodium
364	2g	38g	2g	3g	0mg	289mg

Cajun Sidebar:

If you intend on injecting your meat with this sauce, make sure that you blend the ingredients to remove any lumps so that it easily passes through the injector.

INGREDIENTS	
2	tbsp. finely minced onions
2	tbsp. cane syrup
1/4	tsp. garlic powder
2/8	tsp. cayenne pepper
3	tbsp. fresh lemon juice
1/2	cup Cajun Injector Beef Marinade (Creole Garlic recipe)

BAR-B-QUE SAUCE

Serves 8

This bar-b-que sauce can be injected into meat and also used to baste meat as you cook.

You may substitute the cane syrup with maple syrup or honey.

NUTRITION INFORMATION PER SERVING

Calories	Saturated Fat	Total Fat	Protein	Carbohydrates	Cholesterol	Sodium
14	0g	0g	0.1g	3g	0mg	2mg

Cajun Sidebar:

If you are watching your calories and fat intake, use low-calorie mayonnaise.

INGREDIENTS	
1	cup mayonnaise
2	tsp. sweet pickle relish
1	medium onion, grated

FRONT PORCH TARTAR SAUCE

Serves 8

Mix mayonnaise, pickle relish and grated onion together.

Great with any fried or broiled fish.

NUTRITION INFORMATION PER SERVING

Calories	Saturated Fat	Total Fat	Protein	Carbohydrates	Cholesterol	Sodium
160	2g	14g	0g	7g	0mg	116mg

Cajun Sidebar:

For a different taste, leave skin on potatoes, cut up and boil.

You can also use leftover potatoes from crab or crawfish boils with this recipe.

For the calorie-wise, you can use low-fat or fat-free mayonnaise, and just the whites of the boiled eggs — it's not bad.

INGREDIENTS	
5	lbs. potatoes
2	stalks celery
☞	green onions
6	boiled eggs
6	oz. pickle relish, sweet
1 1/2	cups mayonnaise

JEANNE'S POTATO SALAD

Serves 8

Peel, cut up and boil potatoes until tender. Drain. Add celery, onions, chopped eggs and pickle relish. Mix well. Add mayonnaise. Salt and pepper to taste.

You can eat this while it is still warm or chill in the refrigerator. After serving, chill.

NUTRITION INFORMATION PER SERVING

Calories	Saturated Fat	Total Fat	Protein	Carbohydrates	Cholesterol	Sodium
613	5g	26g	12g	84g	159mg	389mg

Cajun Sidebar:

The next time you have a seafood boil, make a batch of this sauce to dip your seafood and potatoes in.

You can play with this sauce by using more or less of the ingredients.

JB'S POTATO SAUCE

Delicious sauce to spoon over boiled potatoes. Goes great with boiled crawfish or shrimp, too!

INGREDIENTS	
8	fl. oz. Italian salad dressing
3	fl. oz. Cajun Injector Beef Marinade (Creole Garlic recipe)
2	whole, large yellow onions, sliced
1/4	cup cider vinegar
1/2	cup water
1	whole fresh lemon, sliced

Serves 10

Combine all ingredients and simmer on medium heat until onions are wilted and liquid has been reduced about 1/4.

NUTRITION INFORMATION PER SERVING

Calories	Saturated Fat	Total Fat	Protein	Carbohydrates	Cholesterol	Sodium
137	1.6g	11.1g	0.9g	8.4g	0mg	181mg

Cajun Sidebar:

Make up large batches of this sauce and can or freeze for future use. It's also great to give to your relatives!

INGREDIENTS	
2	lbs. onions, chopped
10	oz. cooking oil
6	oz. can tomato paste
24	oz. water (4 - 6 oz. cans)
1	tbsp. mustard
1/4	cup Cajun Injector Beef marinade (Creole Garlic recipe)
16	oz. ketchup
2	tsp. Louisiana-style hot sauce
1/4	cup sugar

Boutte's Eatin' Sauce

A delicious sauce to put on barbeque chicken, pork or beef after it is cooked. So good you might want to eat it on bread!

Serves 15

Sauté onions in cooking oil until wilted. Add tomato paste and cook for several minutes. Add water and blend well. Add remaining ingredients and simmer about 30 minutes — doesn't hurt to cook longer.

Serve on the side of grilled chicken. Wow!

NUTRITION INFORMATION PER SERVING

Calories	Saturated Fat	Total Fat	Protein	Carbohydrates	Cholesterol	Sodium
256	1g	19g	2g	19g	0mg	382mg

SWEETS & TREATS

Cajun Sidebar:

Try serving fresh seasonal berries with this for breakfast, or a scoop of vanilla ice cream with cinnamon apples for a great dessert for a cold, rainy day.

INGREDIENTS	
1/2	cup sugar
3	eggs, beaten
6	slices stale bread
2	tbsp. Grand Marnier (optional)
1	tsp. vanilla
1/2	cup milk
3	tbsp. margarine

FRENCH TOAST (LOST BREAD)

This recipe created one of my fondest childhood memories...a Sunday morning treat after Mass.

Serves 3

Add sugar and vanilla to beaten eggs. Add milk and Grand Marnier (optional). Coat both sides of each slice of bread thoroughly and drop immediately into hot margarine in skillet. Brown on both sides.

Serve with syrup, honey or powdered sugar.

NUTRITION INFORMATION PER SERVING

Calories	Saturated Fat	Total Fat	Protein	Carbohydrates	Cholesterol	Sodium
547	5g	20g	14g	78g	220mg	623mg

Cajun Sidebar:

Bread Pudding is a southern staple. It's a great way to use up day-old French bread. Try using whiskey or liqueurs in place of the rum for a different taste.

Front Porch Bread Pudding

with Rum Sauce

Serve this treat hot. This recipe is easily reheated in the microwave.

INGREDIENTS

BREAD PUDDING:

1	loaf French bread
1	quart milk
4	slightly beaten eggs
2	cups sugar
2	tbsp. vanilla extract
1	cup raisins
3	tbsp. melted butter

RUM SAUCE:

1	stick butter
1	cup sugar
2	fl. oz. rum
1/2	cup water

Serves 10

Soak french bread in the milk for at least one hour. Preheat oven to 350 degrees.

PUDDING: Crush the bread with your hands until it is well mixed with the milk. Add eggs, sugar, vanilla and raisins and stir well. Pour butter into the bottom of a thick, oven-proof pan. Pour batter on top and bake until very firm. Cool pudding before cutting into cubes.

SAUCE: Blend sugar, water and melted butter. Cook until sugar is dissolved. Remove from heat and add rum.

SERVING: Place pudding in individual serving dishes and top with plenty of rum sauce. If necessary, reheat in microwave for approximately 2 minutes, or until heated through.

NUTRITION INFORMATION PER SERVING

Calories	Saturated Fat	Total Fat	Protein	Carbohydrates	Cholesterol	Sodium
520	11g	18g	7g	80g	133mg	223mg

Cajun Sidebar:

This is sure to be a family favorite! Freshly squeezed lemon juice makes the difference with this recipe.

INGREDIENTS	
14	oz. can sweetened condensed milk
3	eggs
3	fresh lemons
1	vanilla wafer pie crust

JEANNE'S LEMON ICE BOX PIE

Easy and delicious.

Serves 8

Separate eggs and add yolks to condensed milk. Blend well. Save egg whites for meringue.

Cut lemons in half, squeezing one half at a time into milk and egg mixture. Stir after each addition. Lemon juice will cook egg yolks, thickening the mixture. Pour into prepared vanilla wafer crust.

Prepare meringue by beating egg whites until stiff. Add two tablespoons of sugar and beat until it takes on a shiny look. Pour on top of pie, making peaks in meringue. Bake at 400 degrees until light brown. Let stand until cool and refrigerate.

NUTRITION INFORMATION PER SERVING

Calories	Saturated Fat	Total Fat	Protein	Carbohydrates	Cholesterol	Sodium
200	3.3g	6.3g	6.5g	29.3g	97mg	88mg

*Nutritional information does not reflect pie crust.

Cajun Sidebar:

Pralines are sold year-round at festivals all over Louisiana. Be careful not to over cook this confection. Use a candy thermometer to get the best results.

INGREDIENTS	
2	cups granulated sugar
1	cup cream
2	tbsp. Karo (light) corn syrup
☞	pinch salt
☞	pinch baking soda
1¼	cups pecan halves

NAWLIN'S CREAMY PRALINES

A rich, creamy candy filled with pecans.

Serves 15

Blend all ingredients except pecans. Stirring continuously, dissolve ingredients over high heat (about 5 minutes). Lower heat, stirring constantly.

Cook to soft-ball stage (238 degrees). This takes about 15 - 20 minutes.

Remove from heat and let stand about 2 minutes. Add pecans and beat until slightly thickened.

Drop by tablespoonfuls onto wax paper.

NUTRITION INFORMATION PER SERVING

Calories	Saturated Fat	Total Fat	Protein	Carbohydrates	Cholesterol	Sodium
221	3.0g	10.5g	1.0g	30.6g	14mg	52mg

Cajun Sidebar:

Leaving on the apple skins is a great way to get more fiber into your diet with this recipe. Although walnuts are our choice, pecans can be substituted.

DIANE'S FRESH APPLE CAKE

INGREDIENTS	
2	cups sugar
$1\frac{1}{2}$	cups vegetable oil
3	eggs, beaten
3	cups flour
1	tsp. salt
$1\frac{1}{2}$	tsp. baking soda
$1\frac{1}{2}$	tsp. vanilla
3	cups apples, unpeeled and diced
1	cup walnuts, chopped
$\frac{3}{4}$	cup coconut

Serves 12

Mix sugar and oil. Add eggs and mix again. Combine flour (plain), salt, soda, and add to sugar mixture. Add vanilla, coconut, apples and walnuts and mix well. Bake at 350 degrees in greased tub pan for about one hour or until toothpick inserted comes out clean.

NUTRITION INFORMATION PER SERVING

Calories	Saturated Fat	Total Fat	Protein	Carbohydrates	Cholesterol	Sodium
641	6g	37g	6g	64g	53mg	317mg

Cajun Sidebar:

The aroma emanating from your kitchen will bring them back for more of this treat. This is one of my favorite recipes, and a true crowd pleaser.

The vinegar is the secret.

INGREDIENTS	
1	stick butter
3	eggs
1	tbsp. vinegar
1 1/2	cups sugar
1	tsp vanilla
1	cup coconut, fresh or frozen

GOOD COCONUT PIE

*And I mean **GOOD** Coconut Pie!*

Serves 8

Mix sugar and butter well, add eggs (one at a time), beat well. Then add vanilla, vinegar and coconut, mixing well.

Pour in unbaked pie shell. Bake 45 minutes at 325 degrees.

NUTRITION INFORMATION PER SERVING

Calories	Saturated Fat	Total Fat	Protein	Carbohydrates	Cholesterol	Sodium
319	11g	17g	3g	39g	111mg	143mg

*Nutritional information does not reflect pie crust.